The Arctic Fox

The Arctic Fox

By Gail LaBonte

DILLON PRESS, INC.
Minneapolis, Minnesota 55415

For my children, Jason and Alison

Acknowledgments

I would like to thank Dr. Erich H. Follmann of the Institute of Arctic Biology at the University of Alaska for the time he spent meeting with me and reading the manuscript for accuracy.

The photographs are reproduced through the courtesy of Fred Bruemmer (pages 2, 8, 14, 24, 26, 29, 33, 34, 39, 49, 51); Dominique Braud/Tom Stack & Associates (page 36); Tim Christie (page 19); Mary Clay/Tom Stack & Associates (page 21); W. Perry Conway/Tom Stack & Associates (page 44); Gerry Ellis/Ellis Wildlife Collection (page 41); Breck P. Kent (pages 23, 46); Leonard Lee Rue III (pages 11, 12); Lynn Stone (pages 16, 31). Cover photo by Fred Bruemmer.

Library of Congress Cataloging-in-Publication Data

LaBonte, Gail.
The arctic fox / by Gail LaBonte.

(A Dillon remarkable animals book)

Includes index.

Summary: Examines the appearance, habitat, and behavior of the arctic fox, discusses its relationship with humans, and describes a year in the life of an arctic fox.

ISBN 0-87518-390-5
1. Arctic fox—Juvenile literature. [1. Arctic fox. 2. Foxes.]
I. Title. II. Series.
QL737.C22L25   1989
599.74'442—dc 19   88-18967
                                                        CIP
                                                        AC

Dillon Press, Inc., 242 Portland Avenue South
Minneapolis, Minnesota 55415

Printed in the United States of America
   2 3 4 5 6 7 8 9 10 98 97 96 95 94 93 92 91 90

Contents

Facts about the Arctic Fox 6

1. The Remarkable Arctic Fox 9

2. A Closer Look 17

3. The Arctic World 27

4. Through the Arctic Year 37

5. The Arctic Fox and People 47

Glossary 55

Index 59

Facts about the Arctic Fox

Scientific Name: *Alopex lagopus*

Varieties: White fox, blue fox

Description:

Length—Of head and body, 20 inches (51 centimeters); of tail, 12 inches (31 centimeters)

Height—12 inches (31 centimeters)

Weight—7 to 15 pounds (3 to 7 kilograms)

Physical Features—Small ears, short nose, oval pupils, bushy tail, furry feet, fur coat which keeps fox warm in temperatures of -40°F (-40°C)

Color—White fox is white in winter, gray-brown in summer; blue fox is smoky gray throughout the year

Distinctive Habits: Travels long distances in search of food; changes diet with seasons and available food; stores extra food in summer to be eaten in winter; stays active through winter; wanders alone except when raising young

Food: Hunts small rodents, such as lemmings and voles, and birds and their eggs; also feeds on dead seals killed by polar bears, caribou and musk oxen killed by wolves, and dead walruses and whales trapped in ice; eats berries and other vegetation in summer

Reproductive Cycle: Female gives birth to a litter of usually five or six pups (sometimes more) between April and June; male helps feed and raise pups; pups leave parents when winter arrives

Range: Throughout the arctic regions of North America, Scandinavia, Asia, on Iceland and the coasts of Greenland, and on islands in the Arctic Ocean and the Bering Sea

The shaded area on this map shows the range of the arctic fox.

Chapter 1

The Remarkable Arctic Fox

Sitting on the sea ice, the arctic fox watches the polar bear from a safe distance. When the time is right, the snow-white fox moves toward the bear. The huge, white bear guards the body of a seal it has killed and dragged from a hole in the ice.

After eating the seal's thick outer layer of fat, the bear is no longer hungry. Still, it is not willing to share. Hissing and growling, it swats a mighty paw at the fox. The small, quick fox springs away from the powerful bear. Boldly, the fox tries again to reach the meat. Again the bear swats at the fox. Finally, tiring of the game, the giant bear ambles off. The fox tears into the seal flesh and eats its fill. It has found the food it needs to survive in a very cold, harsh world.

Searching for food, an arctic fox cautiously approaches a polar bear.

Living in a Cold World

The arctic fox lives in the **Arctic*** near the **North Pole** where, in the winter, the sun never rises and temperatures stay far below freezing. The North Pole lies on a sheet of permanent ice near the center of the Arctic Ocean. Moving sea ice covers this ocean during most of the year. In spring and summer, some of the ice thaws and breaks apart along the northern coasts of North America, Scandinavia, Asia, and most of Greenland's coastline. The lands bordering the Arctic Ocean and the many islands in it make up the "arctic prairie," or **tundra**.

The tundra appears to be a barren land, rocky and treeless. Arctic foxes live in this vast northern region. They are one of the few animals with a **circumpolar** range, meaning they range throughout the areas around the North Pole.

The arctic fox is at home in every part of this frozen territory. It climbs steep, rocky crags on land and trots fearlessly across the sea ice. The fox travels great distances in search of food—some-

*Words in **bold type** are explained in the glossary at the end of this book.

An arctic fox surveys its territory in the frozen land at the top of the world.

The fox's warm coat protects it during the extreme cold of the arctic winter.

times as far as 1,000 miles (1,610 kilometers). Some foxes have even been observed arriving in new areas on **ice floes**, floating ice islands!

Adapting to the Arctic
These animals have developed special features, or **adaptations**, for living in the arctic **environment**.

12

Their fur may be the warmest of all the polar animals. This warm coat protects the arctic fox in the cold winter when it must search constantly for food.

Since the food supply changes with the seasons, the arctic fox has learned to eat a variety of foods. In this way, the fox improves its chances of finding food at all times during the year.

This clever animal even saves food when it is plentiful for times when it is scarce. Late in winter, the arctic fox sometimes fails in its endless hunt for food. Only then will the fox dig up the food it stored during the summer months. This hidden supply is called a **cache** (pronounced *cash*). A Danish scientist once found a fox's cache that contained forty-two birds and a pile of eggs. The birds' heads were bitten off. So far scientists have not been able to explain this unusual behavior.

The native people of the Arctic do have a story to explain the headless birds. They say that long ago the foxes buried the birds whole. But once, a

Using its muzzle, an arctic fox covers a cache which it can use later when food is scarce.

fox hid some birds, and one was not quite dead. In the cold, the bird awakened.

It cried out to the others, "It is cold. We must fly south."

Its voice had magical powers, so all the birds came to life and flew away. From that time on, the story goes, the fox learned to bite off the birds' heads before storing them.

By adapting to its environment, the arctic fox has made the lonely, frozen world at the top of the earth its home. A closer look at the fox's body and behavior shows how well it is suited to life in the far north.

Chapter 2

A Closer Look

Like deer, bears, and humans, foxes are **mammals**. They have fur and feed their babies milk. Mammals such as foxes that eat mostly meat are called **carnivores**. Scientists have divided carnivores into several families, including the cat family, the bear family, and the dog family. Foxes are part of the dog family, also known by its scientific name, **Canidae**. This family includes wolves, coyotes, pet dogs, jackals, and other related animals.

The Foxes

Of all the world's foxes, the red fox is the most common. Its **habitat**, or range, covers large parts of North America, Europe, and Asia. Like the arctic fox, the red fox has been hunted for centuries. Yet

Like other foxes, the arctic fox is a member of the dog family.

it has developed the ability to avoid traps and to live in areas near human communities. The red fox has been found farther and farther north, even in southern parts of the Arctic. When it competes for territory with the smaller arctic fox, the arctic fox usually loses. In some areas of the far north, the arctic fox is being replaced by the red fox.

Other foxes are not as well known as the red fox. The gray fox lives in the area between the northern border of the United States and the northern parts of South America. Among the less common foxes are the swift fox and the kit fox.

The Arctic Fox

The arctic fox is smaller than either the red or the gray fox. This cat-size creature weighs between 7 and 15 pounds (3 and 7 kilograms). In comparison, the wolf, the largest member of the dog family, may weigh 100 pounds (45 kilograms). The head and body of the arctic fox measure about 20 inches (51 centimeters) long, and its bushy tail adds

The arctic fox's small size, compact body, and warm fur are well adapted to its home in the far north.

another foot (31 centimeters) to its length.

The arctic fox has a short nose, short ears, and short legs. Its compact body helps the fox stay warm in the extreme cold of the far north. For example, the fox's small, rounded ears are nearly buried in its fur. If its ears stuck out into the cold air, heat would escape from the animal's body through them. Another kind of fox, the desert kit fox, lives in areas that are extremely hot during most of the year. Its very large, pointed ears allow heat to escape, helping the kit fox to stay cool.

Even the arctic fox's feet are well adapted to its habitat. Its scientific name, *Alopex lagopus*, means "fox with rabbit feet" in Latin. The soles of its feet, like those of the arctic hare and the polar bear, are covered with fur. This thick, warm fur protects the fox's feet while crossing long stretches of ice and snow. On the ice, the fox's sharp claws dig in and keep it from sliding.

The arctic fox's eyes help it adjust to both bright light and the long, dark arctic winter. Its

A close-up view of the eyes of an arctic fox.

yellow eyes look more like a cat's than a dog's because the **pupil**, the dark spot in the center of its eye, is oval instead of round. The pupil opens to let in light. An oval pupil opens very wide to help the fox see better at night. During the day it closes to a thin sliver to shut out the bright light.

As arctic foxes move through their land of ice

and snow, they make a variety of sounds. When they hunt together, the foxes make harsh, croaking barks. They also growl, howl, yelp, and scream. During the spring mating season, the foxes fill the arctic air with their singing.

Fox Fur

There are two **varieties** of arctic fox. Though they are really the same animal, they differ in the color of their fur. All the arctic foxes have coats that are dull brown or gray during the summer. The fur of one variety—the white fox—turns white during the winter. The other variety—the blue fox—remains a blue-gray color throughout the year.

White foxes, which are more common, live on the mainland areas of Canada, Alaska, and Siberia. Blue foxes inhabit the islands and coastal regions of the Arctic Ocean and Greenland. Blue fox fur is more valuable to people than white fox fur. In fact, people have tried to kill all the white foxes in some areas to make room for more blue foxes.

During the winter, the white fur of the arctic fox makes the animal hard to see against the snow and ice.

Long guard hairs and wooly underfur keep the arctic fox's body a toasty 100°F (38°C) no matter how cold it is. In part, its white winter fur serves as **camouflage** to help the fox hunt unseen or hide from enemies on snow and ice. However, the white coat also serves another purpose. It is actually warmer than colored fur.

If the Arctic ever becomes too cold for the fox, it can curl up in the snow and cover its nose with its bushy tail to stay warm.

The color in fur is made by little grains of material called **melanin**. White fur has no melanin. Instead, air fills the spaces in the hair cells where melanin would normally be. Since cold does not pass through this trapped air as well as it passes through solid melanin, white fur keeps the fox warmer. Many other arctic animals have white fur

or feathers to help them survive the cold winter.

The arctic fox roams at temperatures of -40°F (-40°C) without being affected by the cold. If the temperature falls below -40°F, the fox curls up in the snow and covers its nose with its bushy tail. Scientists estimate that even at -100°F (-73°C), the fox would just shiver and use up a little more energy. At the same temperature, a naked person would die within five minutes!

The arctic fox's fur, its small, compact body, and its special feet all help this remarkable animal survive. Its physical features present a strong defense against the extreme cold of its arctic home.

Chapter 3

The Arctic World

Most people will never see the home of the arctic fox. Scientists say the true Arctic begins where the northern forests end. The area where the trees stop and barren plains begin is called the **timberline**. Beyond the timberline, the weather is so severe that trees and plants cannot grow upright. They hug the earth or take shelter between rocks.

Beneath the earth's surface, plant growth is stopped by the frozen ground. In the warmest months, only the top few inches of the ground thaw. Below this thin layer, the earth is permanently frozen. The roots of plants cannot reach into this rock-hard ground, called **permafrost**. Neither the fox or other arctic animals can dig into the permafrost for shelter.

A group of foxes searches for food in the dim light of the arctic sun in late fall.

Arctic Days and Nights

Because of the way the earth tilts, the sun does not rise very high in the arctic sky. During the summer when the North Pole tilts toward the sun, the sun never sets in much of the Arctic. This is called the time of the "midnight sun." Yet, since the sun is low in the sky, it does not give much warmth.

During the winter months, the North Pole tilts away from the sun. Now the sun cannot be seen at all in large parts of the Arctic. Through the long, bitterly cold night, the moon and stars sometimes shine brightly on the snow and ice. As the earth begins to tilt toward the sun again, a dim twilight lightens the arctic world.

Because of the indirect sunlight and the snow and ice, the Arctic reflects more heat into space than it absorbs from the sun. Fortunately, warm ocean currents bring heat to the far north from other parts of the world. Otherwise this polar region would grow colder and colder until all life there would die.

A fox rests on a snow ridge in the last rays of the arctic sun.

The Fox's Neighbors

Since the arctic environment is so harsh, few animals spend the whole year there. Almost all the birds and many of the sea mammals **migrate** to warmer areas for the winter.

Some animals, such as the arctic fox, live year round in the polar region. Several kinds of **rodents** share this winter world and provide food for the fox. Among these rodents are the lemmings and the voles, small mouselike creatures. The arctic hare also stays for the winter, but it is not easy **prey** for the fox.

The wolf, the polar bear, the short-tailed weasel, and the snowy owl are other arctic **predators** that hunt for the scarce food of winter. Each of these animals prefers different foods. In this way they share the available food supply. The wolf hunts for the larger land mammals, such as the musk ox and the caribou. The polar bear feeds on seals and walruses, the mammals of the sea. The weasel and the owl compete with the arctic fox for small animals such as the rodents.

Finding Food

Throughout the year, lemmings are the main food of most arctic foxes. The lemming is a small, furry rodent which burrows under the snow and feeds on arctic plants. Upon hearing a lemming, the fox,

Like the fox, the wolf is a predator that lives year round in the Arctic.

its tail raised, digs furiously through the snow. When it uncovers the lemming, it pounces on it like a cat.

Arctic foxes depend so much on the lemmings for food that as the lemmings increase in number, so do the foxes. Every four years the number of lemmings becomes very large. Such a sudden

31

growth in number is called a population explosion. During this time, the foxes have many pups that grow healthy and fat on the lemmings. Yet their good fortune does not last.

The lemmings are well known for their strange behavior during a population explosion. During the first year of the cycle, there may be only one lemming on each acre (.4 hectare) of tundra. During the second year, there are still just a few. But in the third year, there are many lemmings. And in the fourth year, a mass panic begins among the overcrowded animals. Lemmings run everywhere. Suddenly, they all just want to leave. Many die trying to escape, some by running into the sea and drowning. The next year, when few lemmings remain, many foxes starve to death.

When fresh food is scarce, the fox becomes a **scavenger**, taking the leftovers from other animals. Some arctic foxes follow wolves in hopes of feeding on the remains of caribou and musk ox. But the wolves leave little for the fox, and they may

In late fall and early winter, a fox family may still travel together in search of food such as lemmings.

Arctic foxes follow a polar bear. If the bear kills a seal, the foxes may be able to feed after the bear has eaten its fill.

attack the follower. If the animals are in a rocky area, the sure-footed fox has a chance to escape. On flat ground the wolf can outrun the fox and catch it.

Following a polar bear is often safer and more rewarding for the fox. The polar bear eats only the thick fat underneath the skin of the seal. After

34

eating this **blubber**, the satisfied bear may leave the flesh for a waiting fox.

Traveling across the sea ice, an arctic fox may find the body of a stranded whale or a walrus. Since one large sea mammal provides enough food for many foxes, they come from miles around. Scientists have reported seeing 40 foxes eating a walrus that died when it was trapped in the ice.

Sometimes, the fox fails to find meat. Then it may dig through snow and ice to eat plants or dig up food it has buried in the summer months. The fox may make a pest of itself looking for scraps around the towns of native arctic peoples, scientists' camps, or other human communities. During the winter, the fox must use all its instincts to find food in the frozen arctic world.

Chapter 4

Through the Arctic Year

In late May, when the snow and ice of the tundra melt and the air begins to warm, the female arctic fox, or **vixen**, gives birth to a litter of pups. There are usually five or six pups in a litter. In years when the food supply is large, the vixen may have as many as fifteen pups. The pups are brown and blind at birth and weigh just a few ounces. Their eyes open when they are a week old.

Hungry Pups
At first, the vixen and the pups stay in their den, while the male fox hunts for himself and his mate. He may bring the vixen thirty to forty lemmings each day. When the pups are two weeks old, the vixen leaves them to help with the hunting. Soon

A vixen by its den.

the fox parents begin to feed the baby foxes with half-digested food. At two months of age, the pups stop drinking their mother's milk, and feed on dead animals which the parents bring to the den. Before the pups are ready to hunt for themselves, their parents bring them live animals to kill and eat.

Back and forth through the night and most of the morning, the vixen and her mate hunt lemmings to feed the pups. The litter may eat as many as one hundred lemmings a day! If food is plentiful, all the pups will survive. But if food is scarce, some or all of the pups will die.

When the pups first leave the den, at one month of age, they must beware of the snowy owl and the golden eagle. These large predators sometimes make a meal of the young foxes. At first, the pups play in the sun near the safety of the den.

The Arctic Summer

During the arctic summer, the long days help the growing cycle. The snow melts, but the frozen

During the arctic summer, a fox rests in a meadow in the tundra.

ground cannot absorb the water. Since the water stays on the surface, the tundra becomes a patch-work of streams and ponds. Where the ground is drier, buttercups spread a carpet of bright, yellow flowers, attracting insects.

Many birds that spend the winter months farther south return to the tundra to nest. Thick clouds of insects fill the light arctic sky. Mosquitoes and blackflies hatch in the pools of melted snow. Though the insects are a nuisance to the foxes, they provide food for the birds. The birds, in turn, provide food for the foxes.

As the days grow longer, the arctic fox begins to **molt**, or shed, its warm winter fur. Beginning with the tail, its white coat is replaced by a grayish-brown coat. Now the fox's color matches the gray rocks and the tundra soil. This short summer coat keeps the fox cool in the warmer weather.

In early summer, the fox pups join their parents in hunting. The snow has melted, and the lemming runways are easy to find. Since the pups are awkward at first, they don't catch much. As soon as they learn to imitate their parents' lightning quick pounces, they rarely miss.

The Fox Den

In late summer, when the ground has thawed to the level of the permafrost, arctic foxes work on

Members of a fox family come out of their den.

their dens. Some dens have probably been used for centuries. Yet every year the foxes improve the dens by making them larger and adding new entrances. The foxes pick the easiest digging places for the den, usually under a gravelly mound or in a slope. Dens may have many unfinished burrows where the foxes stopped digging when they reached the permafrost. While the average fox den has four burrows, scientists have found dens with as many as twenty-six entrances. Usually, one fox family lives in each den.

In the summer, dens are easy to spot because the plants grow thick and green around them. The roots grow well in the ground loosened by the foxes' digging, and their droppings fertilize the soil. Scientists search for fox dens from airplanes by looking for areas where the plants grow well.

Preparing for Winter

At the end of summer and beginning of fall, the last abundant food supply of the fox appears on the tundra. Fields of crowberries, bilberries, and mountain cranberries cover the tundra with bright colors. In September, arctic foxes join jaegers and polar bears in harvesting and eating great amounts of these berries.

Then, after a short, colorful fall, the feast ends. Strong winds and storms sweep across the tundra.

Snow falls, and snowdrifts begin to hide the lemmings. The parents no longer assist the young foxes in finding food. Now all the foxes and the other animals that remain compete fiercely for the scarce winter food.

In late October the sun goes down and does not come up again for four months. Soon afterward, the sea's surface freezes in solid sheets of ice. The noise of the crashing waves turns to silence.

Now the fox pups shed their brown fur, and their coats turn white for the first time. Except for their dark eyes and noses, the young foxes are invisible against the background of snow and ice. Their fur grows thick and long to protect the animals against the harsh cold of the arctic winter.

The fox pups spend more and more time away from the den. Eventually they will drift away to look for their own hunting territory. The young foxes may take over the area of an old or injured fox. Sometimes they travel hundreds of miles in search of new territory.

An arctic fox in a winter storm.

For the growing pups, their first arctic winter is a constant struggle to find enough food. The wind blows in gales, swirling the snow into the air. In these conditions human travelers cannot see, and they lose all sense of direction. But the young arctic foxes, with their keen senses, never lose their way. Unbothered by the bitter cold, the foxes travel on in their endless search for food. Before winter ends, many starve or die in traps set by people.

After the sun appears again in February, the days grow longer and longer. By March, the days and nights are of equal length, and by the middle of April, the sun shines at midnight. As the weather warms, the snow and ice begin to melt. During the spring, foxes that have lived through the long winter look for mates. The yearly cycle of life begins again.

Trappers killed many arctic foxes for their valuable pelts.

Chapter 5

The Arctic Fox and People

A starving wolf or polar bear may dig up a fox's den. Golden eagles or snowy owls sometimes steal fox pups. But humans are the arctic fox's greatest enemy.

Long ago, the people of the Arctic trapped only a few foxes. They used the **pelts**, the fur-covered skins, to make parkas and women's pants. The bushy fox tail trimmed the hood of the parka, protecting the wearer's face from cold.

When explorers from other parts of the world came to the Arctic, they discovered the arctic fox and its beautiful fur. Trappers soon followed because they could make money selling fox pelts. In fact, much of the early exploration of the Arctic resulted from the value of the arctic fox's fur. Soon the native peoples also began to sell fox pelts. Thousands of arctic foxes were trapped and killed each year.

Many people object to killing foxes and other animals just for their fur. They worry that these animals will become **extinct**, or disappear completely from the earth. The leopard and the tiger are animals that are threatened with extinction, but so far the arctic fox is not **endangered**. Even though many have been killed, the number of living foxes is still large.

The Future of the Arctic Fox

Just as the fox brought people to the Arctic to make money, natural resources such as oil are now bringing new industries to the far north. Trappers have taken easier, more dependable jobs in these industries. As trappers have turned to other jobs, fox farms have been established where foxes are raised for their furs. People do not hunt the wild arctic fox as much as they once did.

Near an arctic mining camp, an arctic fox takes food from a man's hand.

New industries have meant less fox trapping, but they may cause other hardships for the fox and its animal neighbors. All living things in the Arctic depend on each other for survival. The fox depends on the lemmings. The lemmings, in turn, depend on the arctic plants. Animals and plants linked together in this way are called a **food chain**.

If new construction and road building destroy enough plants, the food chain would be disturbed. When lemmings cannot find enough plants to eat, they starve. Without lemmings, the foxes would starve, too. **Pollution**, dangerous chemicals in the environment, would also break the food chain. If the Arctic Ocean became polluted, many sea birds, sea mammals, and fish would die. Arctic foxes, polar bears, sea mammals, and many birds depend on food from the sea.

Scientists try to prevent activities that would hurt the wildlife or the environment of the Arctic. Sometimes they make careful studies before new industries or construction projects are planned.

One such project is the Alaska pipeline. It was built to carry oil from Prudhoe Bay on the north coast of Alaska to Valdez on the south coast, where it could be loaded onto tanker ships. Since construction began on the pipeline in 1974, scientists have studied the area near the pipeline and the oil drilling at Prudhoe Bay. So far, the animals

Arctic foxes run across the ice. Human activities could harm the food chain that arctic foxes depend upon for survival.

and the environment show little damage from the oil industry.

Some scientists and groups such as the National Wildlife Federation argue that it is too early to tell if these activities are hurting the arctic environment. They believe that officials in government should consider carefully any plans for new arctic industries.

Much more oil has been discovered in an area east of Prudhoe Bay that is now part of Alaska's Arctic National Wildlife Refuge. That discovery raises some hard questions. Should oil companies be allowed to begin drilling in the wildlife refuge? How can the resources of the Arctic be used without destroying the environment? The fox and other arctic animals are sure to be the center of much scientific study, while people decide what to do.

Though the fox is still the most hunted animal in the Arctic, today its numbers may be increasing. The arctic fox is tough. It survives in one of the harshest regions on earth. If we are careful not to harm its environment, this magnificent arctic animal will live for future generations of people to see and admire.

Glossary

adaptations (add-ap-TAY-shuhns)—ways that animals or plants adjust to their surroundings to increase their chances for survival

Arctic—the northern region of the world around the North Pole, including the Arctic Ocean and the northernmost areas of North America, Scandinavia, and Asia

blubber—a thick layer of fat beneath the skin of whales, seals, and other sea mammals

cache (cash)—a hidden supply of food or other goods

camouflage (CAM-uh-flahj)—an appearance, especially color, that blends with the surroundings and may serve to conceal, or hide, an animal

Canidae (CAN-ih-day)—the scientific name for the dog family

carnivore (CAR-nih-vohr)—a flesh-eating animal

circumpolar (sur-cum-POHL-uhr)—completely circling the North or South Pole; the arctic fox has a circumpolar range

endangered—an animal or plant having a population so low it is in danger of becoming extinct

environment—surroundings, including weather conditions, plants, and land features

extinct (ehk-STINGKT)—no longer living anywhere on earth; many plant and animal species have become extinct

food chain—a chain of animals and plants in which each one eats the next; for example, cats eat birds, birds eat insects, and insects eat plants

habitat (HAB-ih-tat)—the region where a plant or animal lives

ice floes—large, flat sheets of ice on the surface of the sea

mammals—warm-blooded animals with backbones and hair; the females bear live young and produce milk to feed them

melanin (MEL-uh-nihn)—a dark brown or black pigment, or color, found in hair, fur, feathers and skin

migrate—to move from one region or climate to another for feeding or breeding; many arctic animals migrate according to the seasons

molt—to shed fur or feathers before they are replaced with new growth

North Pole—the northernmost point of the earth; 90° latitude north

pelt—the fur-covered skin of an animal

permafrost—the permanently frozen ground that lies just a few inches below the surface of the tundra

pollution—any substance that makes water, land, or air dirty or impure

predator (PREHD-uh-tuhr)—an animal that hunts other animals for food

prey—an animal that is hunted by another animal for food

pupil (PYOO-pihl)—the opening in the center of the eye through which light enters

rodent—an animal that gnaws with its front teeth, such as a mouse, rat, or hamster

scavenger (SKA-vuhn-juhr)—an animal that feeds on the remains of dead animals or garbage

timberline—an imaginary line beyond which trees do not grow; in the far north, the timberline marks the beginning of the arctic tundra

tundra (TUHN-druh)—the vast, treeless plains of the Arctic, sometimes called the "arctic prairie"

varieties—animals with distinct characteristics within the same species; the white fox and the blue fox are two varieties of the arctic fox

vixen (VICKS-uhn)—a female fox

Index

adaptations, 12-13
Alaska pipeline, 50-52
Alopex lagopus, 20
Arctic, 10, 27, 28, 47, 49, 50, 52
arctic fox: blue, 22; white, 22
arctic hare, 20, 30
Arctic National Wildlife Refuge, 52
Arctic Ocean, 10, 22, 50
blubber, 34-35
cache, 13, 35
camouflage, 23
Canidae, 17
caribou, 30, 32
carnivores, 17
claws, 20
den, 37, 38, 40-42, 43, 47
desert kit fox, 18, 20
ears, 20
extinction, 48
eyes, 20-21
feet, 20
food, 9, 10, 13, 30, 31, 32-35, 37-38, 40, 42-43, 45
food chain, 49-50

fur, 13, 17, 20, 22-24, 40, 43, 47-48
golden eagle, 38, 47
gray fox, 18
habitat, 17, 20
hunting, 37, 38, 40
ice floes, 12
industries, 49-52
insects, 39-40
jaegers, 42
lemmings, 30-32, 37, 38, 40, 43, 49, 50
litter, 37, 38
mammals, 17, 30, 35, 50
melanin, 24
"midnight sun," 28
migration, 29
molting, 40, 43
musk ox, 30, 32
National Wildlife Federation, 52
North Pole, 10, 28
pelts, 47-48
permafrost, 27, 40, 41-42
polar bear, 9, 20, 30, 34-35, 42, 47

pollution, 50
population explosion, 31-32
predators, 30, 38
prey, 30
pupil, 21
pups, 32, 37-38, 40, 43-45, 47
range, 10, 17, 18, 22
red fox, 17-18
scavenger, 32
sea ice, 9, 10, 43
seals, 9, 30, 34
short-tailed weasel, 30
size, 18-20

snowy owl, 30, 38, 47
sounds, 22
tail, 18-20, 25, 31, 40, 47
territory, 18, 43
timberline, 27
trapping, 47-49
tundra, 10, 37, 39, 40, 42
vixen, 37
voles, 30
walruses, 30, 35
whale, 35
wolves, 17, 18, 30, 32-34, 47

About the Author

As an elementary school teacher in Berkeley, California, Gail LaBonte has shared her love and knowledge of animals with many students. She has studied wildlife firsthand in Africa while assisting her husband in zoological field research. Closer to home in San Francisco, she enjoys observing animals while backpacking or tidepooling along the Pacific Coast with her husband and two children, Jason and Alison. The author is a member of the Society of Children's Book Writers. She is also the author of *The Llama*, another Remarkable Animals book.

EDUCATION